This planner belongs to:

_____

2025

January

S	M	T	W	T	F	S
			1	2	3	4
5	6	7	8	9	10	11
12	13	14	15	16	17	18
19	20	21	22	23	24	25
26	27	28	29	30	31	

February

S	M	T	W	T	F	S
						1
2	3	4	5	6	7	8
9	10	11	12	13	14	15
16	17	18	19	20	21	22
23	24	25	26	27	28	

March

S	M	T	W	T	F	S
						1
2	3	4	5	6	7	8
9	10	11	12	13	14	15
16	17	18	19	20	21	22
23	24	25	26	27	28	29
30	31					

April

S	M	T	W	T	F	S
		1	2	3	4	5
6	7	8	9	10	11	12
13	14	15	16	17	18	19
20	21	22	23	24	25	26
27	28	29	30			

May

S	M	T	W	T	F	S
				1	2	3
4	5	6	7	8	9	10
11	12	13	14	15	16	17
18	19	20	21	22	23	24
25	26	27	28	29	30	31

June

S	M	T	W	T	F	S
1	2	3	4	5	6	7
8	9	10	11	12	13	14
15	16	17	18	19	20	21
22	23	24	25	26	27	28
29	30					

July

S	M	T	W	T	F	S
		1	2	3	4	5
6	7	8	9	10	11	12
13	14	15	16	17	18	19
20	21	22	23	24	25	26
27	28	29	30	31		

August

S	M	T	W	T	F	S
					1	2
3	4	5	6	7	8	9
10	11	12	13	14	15	16
17	18	19	20	21	22	23
24	25	26	27	28	29	30
31						

September

S	M	T	W	T	F	S
	1	2	3	4	5	6
7	8	9	10	11	12	13
14	15	16	17	18	19	20
21	22	23	24	25	26	27
28	29	30				

October

S	M	T	W	T	F	S
			1	2	3	4
5	6	7	8	9	10	11
12	13	14	15	16	17	18
19	20	21	22	23	24	25
26	27	28	29	30	31	

November

S	M	T	W	T	F	S
						1
2	3	4	5	6	7	8
9	10	11	12	13	14	15
16	17	18	19	20	21	22
23	24	25	26	27	28	29
30						

December

S	M	T	W	T	F	S
	1	2	3	4	5	6
7	8	9	10	11	12	13
14	15	16	17	18	19	20
21	22	23	24	25	26	27
28	29	30	31			

Year in Pixels

	J	F	M	A	M	J	J	A	S	O	N	D
1.												
2.												
3.												
4.												
5.												
6.												
7.												
8.												
9.												
10.												
11.												
12.												
13.												
14.												
15.												
16.												
17.												
18.												
19.												
20.												
21.												
22.												
23.												
24.												
25.												
26.												
27.												
28.												
29.												
30.												
31.												

Color Codes

Notes

January 2025

MONDAY	TUESDAY	WEDNESDAY	THURSDAY
		1	2
6	7	8	9
13	14	15	16
20	21	22	23
27	28	29	30

January

2025

FRIDAY	SATURDAY	SUNDAY	NOTES
3	4	5	○
			○
			○
			○
			○
10	11	12	○
			○
			○
			○
17	18	19	○
			○
			○
			○
			○
24	25	26	○
			○
			○
			○
			○
31			NOTES

February 2025

MONDAY	TUESDAY	WEDNESDAY	THURSDAY
3	4	5	6
10	11	12	13
17	18	19	20
24	25	26	27

February

FRIDAY	SATURDAY	SUNDAY	NOTES
	1	2	○
			○
			○
			○
			○
7	8	9	○
			○
			○
			○
			○
14	15	16	○
			○
			○
			○
			○
21	22	23	○
			○
			○
			○
			○
28			NOTES

March

MONDAY	TUESDAY	WEDNESDAY	THURSDAY
		1	2
6	7	8	9
13	14	15	16
20	21	22	23
27	28	29	30

March

FRIDAY	SATURDAY	SUNDAY	NOTES
3	4	5	○
			○
			○
			○
			○
10	11	12	○
			○
			○
			○
17	18	19	○
			○
			○
			○
			○
24	25	26	○
			○
			○
			○
			○
31			NOTES

April 2025

MONDAY	TUESDAY	WEDNESDAY	THURSDAY
	1	2	3
7	8	9	10
14	15	16	17
21	22	23	24
28	29	30	

April

FRIDAY	SATURDAY	SUNDAY	NOTES
4	5	6	○
			○
			○
			○
			○
11	12	13	○
			○
			○
			○
18	19	20	○
			○
			○
			○
			○
25	26	27	○
			○
			○
			○
			○
			NOTES

May

MONDAY	TUESDAY	WEDNESDAY	THURSDAY
			1
5	6	7	8
12	13	14	15
19	20	21	22
26	27	28	29

May

2025

FRIDAY	SATURDAY	SUNDAY	NOTES
2	3	4	○
			○
			○
			○
			○
9	10	11	○
			○
			○
			○
			○
16	17	18	○
			○
			○
			○
23	24	25	○
			○
			○
			○
			○
30	31		NOTES

June 2025

MONDAY	TUESDAY	WEDNESDAY	THURSDAY
2	3	4	5
9	10	11	12
16	17	18	19
23	24	25	26

June 2025

FRIDAY	SATURDAY	SUNDAY	NOTES
		1	○
			○
			○
			○
			○
6	7	8	○
			○
			○
			○
			○
13	14	15	○
			○
			○
			○
			○
20	21	22	○
			○
			○
			○
			○
27	28	29	30

July

MONDAY	TUESDAY	WEDNESDAY	THURSDAY
	1	2	3
7	8	9	10
14	15	16	17
21	22	23	24
28	29	30	31

July

FRIDAY	SATURDAY	SUNDAY	NOTES
4	5	6	○
			○
			○
			○
			○
11	12	13	○
			○
			○
			○
			○
18	19	20	○
			○
			○
			○
			○
25	26	27	○
			○
			○
			○
			○
			NOTES

August

MONDAY	TUESDAY	WEDNESDAY	THURSDAY
4	5	6	7
11	12	13	14
18	19	20	21
25	26	27	28

August

2025

FRIDAY	SATURDAY	SUNDAY	NOTES
1	2	3	○
			○
			○
			○
8	9	10	○
			○
			○
			○
15	16	17	○
			○
			○
			○
			○
22	23	24	NOTES
29	30	31	

September

MONDAY	TUESDAY	WEDNESDAY	THURSDAY
1	2	3	4
8	9	10	11
15	16	17	18
22	23	24	25
29	30		

September

FRIDAY	SATURDAY	SUNDAY	NOTES
5	6	7	○
			○
			○
			○
			○
12	13	14	○
			○
			○
			○
			○
19	20	21	○
			○
			○
			○
			○
26	27	28	○
			○
			○
			○
			○
			NOTES

October

MONDAY	TUESDAY	WEDNESDAY	THURSDAY
		1	2
6	7	8	9
13	14	15	16
20	21	22	23
27	28	29	30

October

2025

FRIDAY	SATURDAY	SUNDAY	NOTES
3	4	5	○
			○
			○
			○
			○
10	11	12	○
			○
			○
			○
17	18	19	○
			○
			○
			○
			○
24	25	26	○
			○
			○
			○
			○
31			NOTES

November 2025

MONDAY	TUESDAY	WEDNESDAY	THURSDAY
3	4	5	6
10	11	12	13
17	18	19	20
24	25	26	27

November

2025

FRIDAY	SATURDAY	SUNDAY	NOTES
	1	2	○
			○
			○
			○
			○
7	8	9	○
			○
			○
			○
14	15	16	○
			○
			○
			○
			○
21	22	23	○
			○
			○
			○
			○
28	29	30	NOTES

December

2025

THURSDAY	TUESDAY	WEDNESDAY	THURSDAY
1	2	3	4
8	9	10	11
15	16	17	18
22	23	24	25
29	30	31	

December

FRIDAY	SATURDAY	SUNDAY	NOTES
5	6	7	○
			○
			○
			○
			○
12	13	14	○
			○
			○
			○
19	20	21	○
			○
			○
			○
			○
26	27	28	○
			○
			○
			○
			○
			NOTES

December
2024

01 SUNDAY

○
○
○
○
○
○
○

02 MONDAY

○
○
○
○
○
○
○
○

03 TUESDAY

○
○
○
○
○
○
○
○

04 WEDNESDAY

○
○
○
○
○

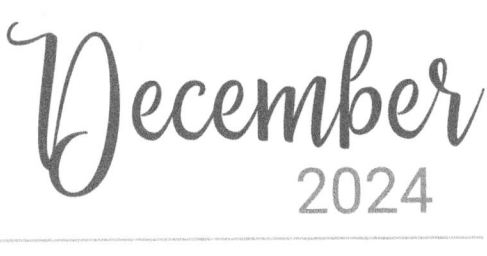

December
2024

05 THURSDAY

○
○
○
○
○
○
○
○

06 FRIDAY

○
○
○
○
○
○
○
○

07 SATURDAY

○
○
○
○
○
○
○
○

08 SUNDAY

○
○
○
○
○

December
2024

09 MONDAY

○ _____
○ _____
○ _____
○ _____
○ _____
○ _____
○ _____
○ _____

10 TUESDAY

○ _____
○ _____
○ _____
○ _____
○ _____
○ _____
○ _____
○ _____

11 WEDNESDAY

○ _____
○ _____
○ _____
○ _____
○ _____
○ _____
○ _____
○ _____

12 THURSDAY

○ _____
○ _____
○ _____
○ _____
○ _____

13 FRIDAY

○
○
○
○
○
○
○

14 SATURDAY

○
○
○
○
○
○
○
○

15 SUNDAY

○
○
○
○
○
○
○
○

16 MONDAY

○
○
○
○
○

17 TUESDAY

18 WEDNESDAY

19 THURSDAY

20 FRIDAY

21 SATURDAY

○
○
○
○
○
○
○
○

22 SUNDAY

○
○
○
○
○
○
○
○

23 MONDAY

○
○
○
○
○
○
○
○

24 TUESDAY

○
○
○
○
○

25 WEDNESDAY

26 THURSDAY

27 FRIDAY

28 SATURDAY

December
2024

29 SUNDAY

30 MONDAY

31 TUESDAY

NOTES

January
2025

01 WEDNESDAY

02 THURSDAY

03 FRIDAY

04 SATURDAY

05 SUNDAY

○ _____
○ _____
○ _____
○ _____
○ _____
○ _____
○ _____

06 MONDAY

○ _____
○ _____
○ _____
○ _____
○ _____
○ _____
○ _____
○ _____

07 TUESDAY

○ _____
○ _____
○ _____
○ _____
○ _____
○ _____
○ _____
○ _____

08 WEDNESDAY

○ _____
○ _____
○ _____
○ _____
○ _____

January
2025

09 THURSDAY

10 FRIDAY

11 SATURDAY

12 SUNDAY

13 MONDAY

○
○
○
○
○
○
○
○

14 TUESDAY

○
○
○
○
○
○
○
○

15 WEDNESDAY

○
○
○
○
○
○
○
○

16 THURSDAY

○
○
○
○
○

17 FRIDAY

○ _____
○ _____
○ _____
○ _____
○ _____
○ _____
○ _____
○ _____

18 SATURDAY

○ _____
○ _____
○ _____
○ _____
○ _____
○ _____
○ _____
○ _____

19 SUNDAY

○ _____
○ _____
○ _____
○ _____
○ _____
○ _____
○ _____
○ _____

20 MONDAY

○ _____
○ _____
○ _____
○ _____
○ _____

21 TUESDAY

○
○
○
○
○
○
○
○

22 WEDNESDAY

○
○
○
○
○
○
○
○
○

23 THURSDAY

○
○
○
○
○
○
○
○
○

24 FRIDAY

○
○
○
○
○

25 SATURDAY

○ _____
○ _____
○ _____
○ _____
○ _____
○ _____
○ _____
○ _____

26 SUNDAY

○ _____
○ _____
○ _____
○ _____
○ _____
○ _____
○ _____
○ _____

27 MONDAY

○ _____
○ _____
○ _____
○ _____
○ _____
○ _____
○ _____
○ _____

28 TUESDAY

○ _____
○ _____
○ _____
○ _____
○ _____

January
2025

29 WEDNESDAY

○ _____
○ _____
○ _____
○ _____
○ _____
○ _____
○ _____
○ _____

30 THURSDAY

○ _____
○ _____
○ _____
○ _____
○ _____
○ _____
○ _____
○ _____

31 FRIDAY

○ _____
○ _____
○ _____
○ _____
○ _____
○ _____
○ _____
○ _____

NOTES

_____
_____
_____
_____

February
2025

01 SATURDAY
○ _____
○ _____
○ _____
○ _____
○ _____
○ _____
○ _____
○ _____

02 SUNDAY
○ _____
○ _____
○ _____
○ _____
○ _____
○ _____
○ _____
○ _____

03 MONDAY
○ _____
○ _____
○ _____
○ _____
○ _____
○ _____
○ _____
○ _____

04 TUESDAY
○ _____
○ _____
○ _____
○ _____
○ _____

05 WEDNESDAY

○ ──────────────────────────────────────
○ ──────────────────────────────────────
○ ──────────────────────────────────────
○ ──────────────────────────────────────
○ ──────────────────────────────────────
○ ──────────────────────────────────────
○ ──────────────────────────────────────
○ ──────────────────────────────────────

06 THURSDAY

○ ──────────────────────────────────────
○ ──────────────────────────────────────
○ ──────────────────────────────────────
○ ──────────────────────────────────────
○ ──────────────────────────────────────
○ ──────────────────────────────────────
○ ──────────────────────────────────────
○ ──────────────────────────────────────

07 FRIDAY

○ ──────────────────────────────────────
○ ──────────────────────────────────────
○ ──────────────────────────────────────
○ ──────────────────────────────────────
○ ──────────────────────────────────────
○ ──────────────────────────────────────
○ ──────────────────────────────────────
○ ──────────────────────────────────────

08 SATURDAY

○ ──────────────────────────────────────
○ ──────────────────────────────────────
○ ──────────────────────────────────────
○ ──────────────────────────────────────
○ ──────────────────────────────────────

09 SUNDAY

○
○
○
○
○
○
○

10 MONDAY

○
○
○
○
○
○
○
○

11 TUESDAY

○
○
○
○
○
○
○
○

12 WEDNESDAY

○
○
○
○
○

February
2025

13 THURSDAY
○
○
○
○
○
○
○
○

14 FRIDAY
○
○
○
○
○
○
○
○

15 SATURDAY
○
○
○
○
○
○
○
○

16 SUNDAY
○
○
○
○
○

17 MONDAY

18 TUESDAY

19 WEDNESDAY

20 THURSDAY

February
2025

21 FRIDAY

○
○
○
○
○
○
○
○

22 SATURDAY

○
○
○
○
○
○
○
○

23 SUNDAY

○
○
○
○
○
○
○
○

24 MONDAY

○
○
○
○
○

February
2025

25 TUESDAY

○
○
○
○
○
○
○
○

26 WEDNESDAY

○
○
○
○
○
○
○
○

27 THURSDAY

○
○
○
○
○
○
○
○

28 FRIDAY

○
○
○
○
○

March
2025

01 SATURDAY

○
○
○
○
○
○
○

02 SUNDAY

○
○
○
○
○
○
○
○

03 MONDAY

○
○
○
○
○
○
○
○

04 TUESDAY

○
○
○
○
○

March
2025

05 WEDNESDAY

○ _____
○ _____
○ _____
○ _____
○ _____
○ _____
○ _____
○ _____

06 THURSDAY

○ _____
○ _____
○ _____
○ _____
○ _____
○ _____
○ _____
○ _____

07 FRIDAY

○ _____
○ _____
○ _____
○ _____
○ _____
○ _____
○ _____
○ _____

08 SATURDAY

○ _____
○ _____
○ _____
○ _____
○ _____

09 SUNDAY

10 MONDAY

11 TUESDAY

12 WEDNESDAY

13 THURSDAY

14 FRIDAY

15 SATURDAY

16 SUNDAY

17 MONDAY

○
○
○
○
○
○
○
○

18 TUESDAY

○
○
○
○
○
○
○
○
○

19 WEDNESDAY

○
○
○
○
○
○
○
○

20 THURSDAY

○
○
○
○
○

21 FRIDAY

22 SATURDAY

23 SUNDAY

24 MONDAY

25 TUESDAY

26 WEDNESDAY

27 THURSDAY

28 FRIDAY

29 SATURDAY

30 SUNDAY

31 MONDAY

NOTES

April 2025

01 TUESDAY

02 WEDNESDAY

03 THURSDAY

04 FRIDAY

05 SATURDAY

06 SUNDAY

07 MONDAY

08 TUESDAY

April
2025

09 WEDNESDAY

10 THURSDAY

11 FRIDAY

12 SATURDAY

April 2025

13 SUNDAY
- ○ _____
- ○ _____
- ○ _____
- ○ _____
- ○ _____
- ○ _____
- ○ _____
- ○ _____

14 MONDAY
- ○ _____
- ○ _____
- ○ _____
- ○ _____
- ○ _____
- ○ _____
- ○ _____
- ○ _____

15 TUESDAY
- ○ _____
- ○ _____
- ○ _____
- ○ _____
- ○ _____
- ○ _____
- ○ _____
- ○ _____

16 WEDNESDAY
- ○ _____
- ○ _____
- ○ _____
- ○ _____
- ○ _____

17 THURSDAY

18 FRIDAY

19 SATURDAY

20 SUNDAY

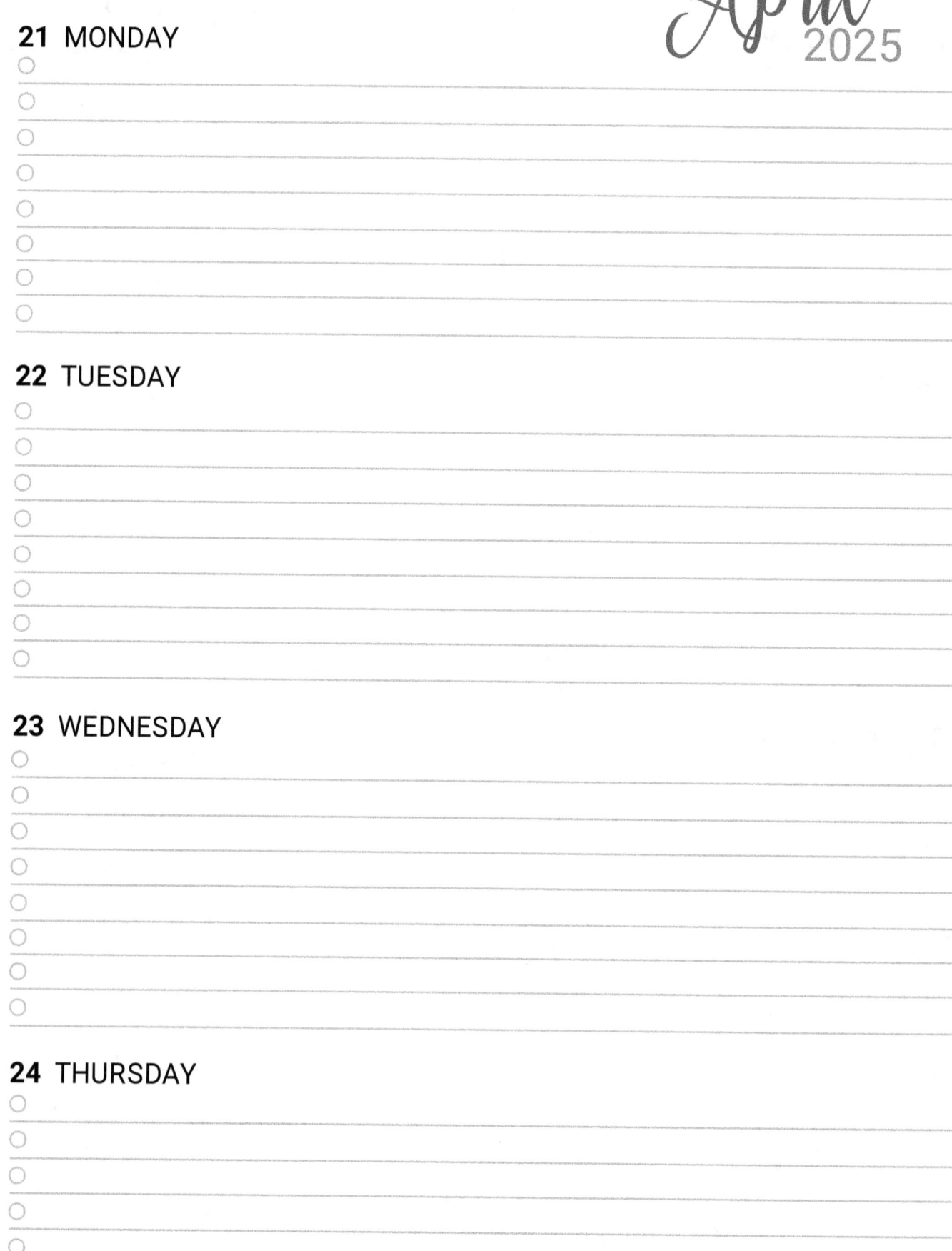

21 MONDAY

22 TUESDAY

23 WEDNESDAY

24 THURSDAY

April 2025

25 FRIDAY

26 SATURDAY

27 SUNDAY

28 MONDAY

29 TUESDAY

○ _____
○ _____
○ _____
○ _____
○ _____
○ _____
○ _____
○ _____

30 WEDNESDAY

○ _____
○ _____
○ _____
○ _____
○ _____
○ _____
○ _____
○ _____

NOTES

_____
_____
_____
_____
_____
_____
_____
_____
_____
_____
_____

May
2025

01 THURSDAY

02 FRIDAY

03 SATURDAY

04 SUNDAY

May 2025

05 MONDAY

06 TUESDAY

07 WEDNESDAY

08 THURSDAY

May
2025

09 FRIDAY

○
○
○
○
○
○
○
○

10 SATURDAY

○
○
○
○
○
○
○
○
○

11 SUNDAY

○
○
○
○
○
○
○
○

12 MONDAY

○
○
○
○
○

13 TUESDAY

14 WEDNESDAY

15 THURSDAY

16 FRIDAY

17 SATURDAY

○ _____
○ _____
○ _____
○ _____
○ _____
○ _____
○ _____

18 SUNDAY

○ _____
○ _____
○ _____
○ _____
○ _____
○ _____
○ _____
○ _____

19 MONDAY

○ _____
○ _____
○ _____
○ _____
○ _____
○ _____
○ _____
○ _____

20 TUESDAY

○ _____
○ _____
○ _____
○ _____
○ _____

21 WEDNESDAY

○
○
○
○
○
○
○
○

22 THURSDAY

○
○
○
○
○
○
○
○

23 FRIDAY

○
○
○
○
○
○
○
○

24 SATURDAY

○
○
○
○
○

May
2025

25 SUNDAY

26 MONDAY

27 TUESDAY

28 WEDNESDAY

29 THURSDAY

○
○
○
○
○
○
○
○

30 FRIDAY

○
○
○
○
○
○
○
○

31 SATURDAY

○
○
○
○
○
○
○
○

NOTES

01 SUNDAY

○ _____
○ _____
○ _____
○ _____
○ _____
○ _____
○ _____

02 MONDAY

○ _____
○ _____
○ _____
○ _____
○ _____
○ _____
○ _____

03 TUESDAY

○ _____
○ _____
○ _____
○ _____
○ _____
○ _____
○ _____
○ _____

04 WEDNESDAY

○ _____
○ _____
○ _____
○ _____
○ _____

05 THURSDAY

06 FRIDAY

07 SATURDAY

08 SUNDAY

June 2025

09 MONDAY

10 TUESDAY

11 WEDNESDAY

12 THURSDAY

13 FRIDAY

○
○
○
○
○
○
○
○

14 SATURDAY

○
○
○
○
○
○
○
○

15 SUNDAY

○
○
○
○
○
○
○
○

16 MONDAY

○
○
○
○
○

17 TUESDAY

○ _____
○ _____
○ _____
○ _____
○ _____
○ _____
○ _____
○ _____

18 WEDNESDAY

○ _____
○ _____
○ _____
○ _____
○ _____
○ _____
○ _____
○ _____

19 THURSDAY

○ _____
○ _____
○ _____
○ _____
○ _____
○ _____
○ _____
○ _____

20 FRIDAY

○ _____
○ _____
○ _____
○ _____
○ _____

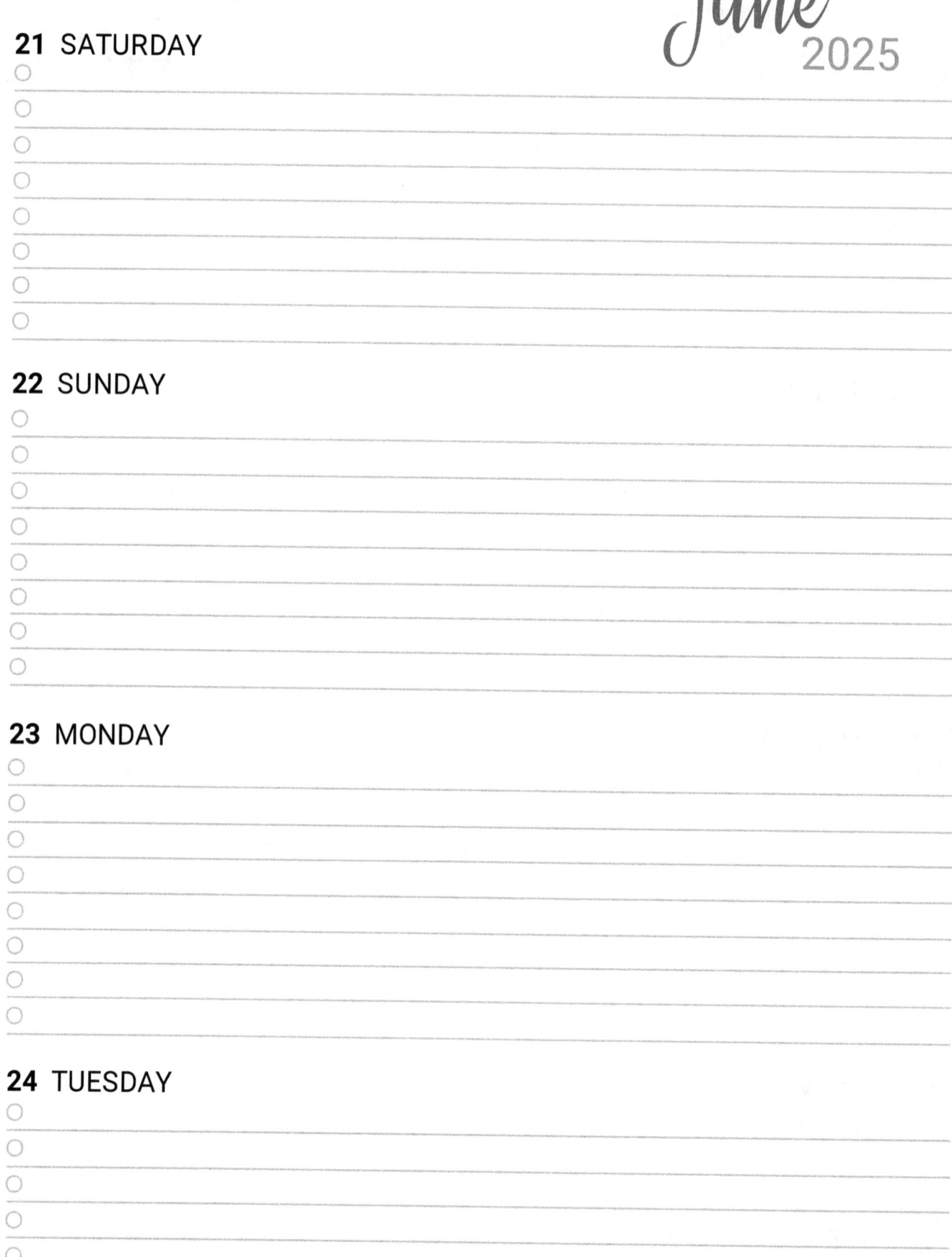

June
2025

21 SATURDAY

22 SUNDAY

23 MONDAY

24 TUESDAY

25 WEDNESDAY

○ _____
○ _____
○ _____
○ _____
○ _____
○ _____
○ _____
○ _____

26 THURSDAY

○ _____
○ _____
○ _____
○ _____
○ _____
○ _____
○ _____
○ _____

27 FRIDAY

○ _____
○ _____
○ _____
○ _____
○ _____
○ _____
○ _____
○ _____

28 SATURDAY

○ _____
○ _____
○ _____
○ _____
○ _____

29 SUNDAY

○ _____
○ _____
○ _____
○ _____
○ _____
○ _____
○ _____
○ _____

30 MONDAY

○ _____
○ _____
○ _____
○ _____
○ _____
○ _____
○ _____
○ _____

NOTES

_____
_____
_____
_____
_____
_____
_____
_____
_____
_____

July
2025

01 TUESDAY

○
○
○
○
○
○
○
○

02 WEDNESDAY

○
○
○
○
○
○
○
○

03 THURSDAY

○
○
○
○
○
○
○
○

04 FRIDAY

○
○
○
○
○

05 SATURDAY

06 SUNDAY

07 MONDAY

08 TUESDAY

July
2025

09 WEDNESDAY

10 THURSDAY

11 FRIDAY

12 SATURDAY

13 SUNDAY

○ _____
○ _____
○ _____
○ _____
○ _____
○ _____
○ _____
○ _____

14 MONDAY

○ _____
○ _____
○ _____
○ _____
○ _____
○ _____
○ _____
○ _____

15 TUESDAY

○ _____
○ _____
○ _____
○ _____
○ _____
○ _____
○ _____
○ _____

16 WEDNESDAY

○ _____
○ _____
○ _____
○ _____
○ _____

July
2025

17 THURSDAY

18 FRIDAY

19 SATURDAY

20 SUNDAY

21 MONDAY
- ○
- ○
- ○
- ○
- ○
- ○
- ○
- ○

22 TUESDAY
- ○
- ○
- ○
- ○
- ○
- ○
- ○
- ○

23 WEDNESDAY
- ○
- ○
- ○
- ○
- ○
- ○
- ○
- ○

24 THURSDAY
- ○
- ○
- ○
- ○
- ○

July
2025

25 FRIDAY
○
○
○
○
○
○
○
○

26 SATURDAY
○
○
○
○
○
○
○
○

27 SUNDAY
○
○
○
○
○
○
○
○

28 MONDAY
○
○
○
○
○

July

2025

29 TUESDAY
- ○
- ○
- ○
- ○
- ○
- ○
- ○
- ○

30 WEDNESDAY
- ○
- ○
- ○
- ○
- ○
- ○
- ○
- ○

31 THURSDAY
- ○
- ○
- ○
- ○
- ○
- ○
- ○
- ○

NOTES

August
2025

01 FRIDAY

○ _____
○ _____
○ _____
○ _____
○ _____
○ _____
○ _____
○ _____

02 SATURDAY

○ _____
○ _____
○ _____
○ _____
○ _____
○ _____
○ _____
○ _____

03 SUNDAY

○ _____
○ _____
○ _____
○ _____
○ _____
○ _____
○ _____
○ _____

04 MONDAY

○ _____
○ _____
○ _____
○ _____
○ _____

05 TUESDAY

○
○
○
○
○
○
○
○

06 WEDNESDAY

○
○
○
○
○
○
○
○

07 THURSDAY

○
○
○
○
○
○
○
○

08 FRIDAY

○
○
○
○
○

August
2025

09 SATURDAY

10 SUNDAY

11 MONDAY

12 TUESDAY

13 WEDNESDAY

14 THURSDAY

15 FRIDAY

16 SATURDAY

17 SUNDAY

18 MONDAY

19 TUESDAY

20 WEDNESDAY

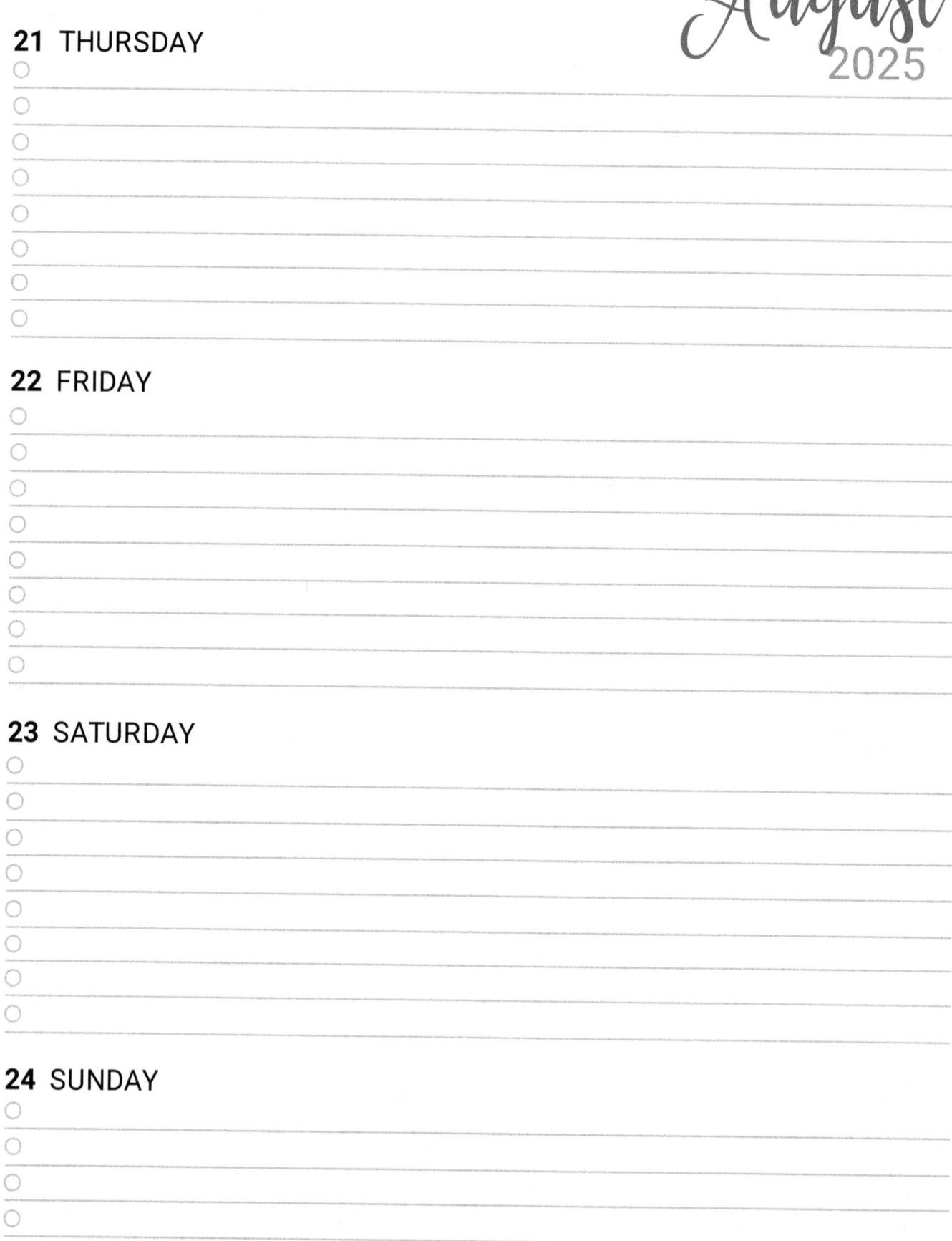

August
2025

21 THURSDAY

22 FRIDAY

23 SATURDAY

24 SUNDAY

August
2025

25 MONDAY

26 TUESDAY

27 WEDNESDAY

28 THURSDAY

29 FRIDAY

30 SATURDAY

31 SUNDAY

NOTES

September
2025

01 MONDAY

○ ....
○ ....
○ ....
○ ....
○ ....
○ ....
○ ....
○ ....

02 TUESDAY

○ ....
○ ....
○ ....
○ ....
○ ....
○ ....
○ ....
○ ....

03 WEDNESDAY

○ ....
○ ....
○ ....
○ ....
○ ....
○ ....
○ ....
○ ....

04 THURSDAY

○ ....
○ ....
○ ....
○ ....
○ ....

September
2025

05 FRIDAY
- ○
- ○
- ○
- ○
- ○
- ○
- ○
- ○

06 SATURDAY
- ○
- ○
- ○
- ○
- ○
- ○
- ○
- ○

07 SUNDAY
- ○
- ○
- ○
- ○
- ○
- ○
- ○
- ○

08 MONDAY
- ○
- ○
- ○
- ○
- ○

09 TUESDAY

○ _____
○ _____
○ _____
○ _____
○ _____
○ _____
○ _____
○ _____

10 WEDNESDAY

○ _____
○ _____
○ _____
○ _____
○ _____
○ _____
○ _____
○ _____

11 THURSDAY

○ _____
○ _____
○ _____
○ _____
○ _____
○ _____
○ _____
○ _____

12 FRIDAY

○ _____
○ _____
○ _____
○ _____
○ _____

13 SATURDAY

○
○
○
○
○
○
○
○

14 SUNDAY

○
○
○
○
○
○
○
○

15 MONDAY

○
○
○
○
○
○
○
○

16 TUESDAY

○
○
○
○
○

17 WEDNESDAY

○
○
○
○
○
○
○
○

18 THURSDAY

○
○
○
○
○
○
○
○

19 FRIDAY

○
○
○
○
○
○
○
○

20 SATURDAY

○
○
○
○
○

21 SUNDAY
- ○
- ○
- ○
- ○
- ○
- ○
- ○
- ○

22 MONDAY
- ○
- ○
- ○
- ○
- ○
- ○
- ○
- ○

23 TUESDAY
- ○
- ○
- ○
- ○
- ○
- ○
- ○
- ○

24 WEDNESDAY
- ○
- ○
- ○
- ○
- ○

25 THURSDAY
○
○
○
○
○
○
○
○

26 FRIDAY
○
○
○
○
○
○
○
○

27 SATURDAY
○
○
○
○
○
○
○
○

28 SUNDAY
○
○
○
○
○

29 MONDAY

○
○
○
○
○
○
○
○

30 TUESDAY

○
○
○
○
○
○
○
○

NOTES

October
2025

01 WEDNESDAY

02 THURSDAY

03 FRIDAY

04 SATURDAY

October
2025

05 SUNDAY

06 MONDAY

07 TUESDAY

08 WEDNESDAY

09 THURSDAY

10 FRIDAY

11 SATURDAY

12 SUNDAY

October
2025

13 MONDAY

○
○
○
○
○
○
○

14 TUESDAY

○
○
○
○
○
○
○
○

15 WEDNESDAY

○
○
○
○
○
○
○
○

16 THURSDAY

○
○
○
○
○

October
2025

17 FRIDAY

○
○
○
○
○
○
○
○

18 SATURDAY

○
○
○
○
○
○
○
○
○

19 SUNDAY

○
○
○
○
○
○
○
○

20 MONDAY

○
○
○
○
○

21 TUESDAY

22 WEDNESDAY

23 THURSDAY

24 FRIDAY

October
2025

25 SATURDAY
○
○
○
○
○
○
○
○

26 SUNDAY
○
○
○
○
○
○
○
○

27 MONDAY
○
○
○
○
○
○
○
○

28 TUESDAY
○
○
○
○
○

October
2025

29 WEDNESDAY

○ _____
○ _____
○ _____
○ _____
○ _____
○ _____
○ _____
○ _____

30 THURSDAY

○ _____
○ _____
○ _____
○ _____
○ _____
○ _____
○ _____
○ _____

31 FRIDAY

○ _____
○ _____
○ _____
○ _____
○ _____
○ _____
○ _____
○ _____

NOTES

_____
_____
_____
_____
_____

01 SATURDAY

○
○
○
○
○
○
○
○

02 SUNDAY

○
○
○
○
○
○
○
○

03 MONDAY

○
○
○
○
○
○
○
○

04 TUESDAY

○
○
○
○
○

05 WEDNESDAY

○
○
○
○
○
○
○
○

06 THURSDAY

○
○
○
○
○
○
○
○

07 FRIDAY

○
○
○
○
○
○
○
○

08 SATURDAY

○
○
○
○
○

09 SUNDAY

10 MONDAY

11 TUESDAY

12 WEDNESDAY

13 THURSDAY

14 FRIDAY

15 SATURDAY

16 SUNDAY

November
2025

17 MONDAY

○ _____
○ _____
○ _____
○ _____
○ _____
○ _____
○ _____

18 TUESDAY

○ _____
○ _____
○ _____
○ _____
○ _____
○ _____
○ _____

19 WEDNESDAY

○ _____
○ _____
○ _____
○ _____
○ _____
○ _____
○ _____

20 THURSDAY

○ _____
○ _____
○ _____
○ _____
○ _____

21 FRIDAY

○
○
○
○
○
○
○
○

22 SATURDAY

○
○
○
○
○
○
○
○

23 SUNDAY

○
○
○
○
○
○
○
○

24 MONDAY

○
○
○
○
○

November
2025

25 TUESDAY
○
○
○
○
○
○
○
○

26 WEDNESDAY
○
○
○
○
○
○
○
○

27 THURSDAY
○
○
○
○
○
○
○
○

28 FRIDAY
○
○
○
○
○

November
2025

29 SATURDAY

○ _____
○ _____
○ _____
○ _____
○ _____
○ _____
○ _____
○ _____

30 SUNDAY

○ _____
○ _____
○ _____
○ _____
○ _____
○ _____
○ _____
○ _____

NOTES

_____
_____
_____
_____
_____
_____
_____
_____
_____
_____
_____
_____

December
2025

01 MONDAY

○
○
○
○
○
○
○

02 TUESDAY

○
○
○
○
○
○
○
○

03 WEDNESDAY

○
○
○
○
○
○
○
○

04 THURSDAY

○
○
○
○
○

December
2025

05 FRIDAY

06 SATURDAY

07 SUNDAY

08 MONDAY

09 TUESDAY

10 WEDNESDAY

11 THURSDAY

12 FRIDAY

13 SATURDAY

14 SUNDAY

15 MONDAY

16 TUESDAY

17 WEDNESDAY

18 THURSDAY

19 FRIDAY

20 SATURDAY

December
2025

21 SUNDAY

22 MONDAY

23 TUESDAY

24 WEDNESDAY

25 THURSDAY

○
○
○
○
○
○
○
○

26 FRIDAY

○
○
○
○
○
○
○
○

27 SATURDAY

○
○
○
○
○
○
○
○

28 SUNDAY

○
○
○
○
○

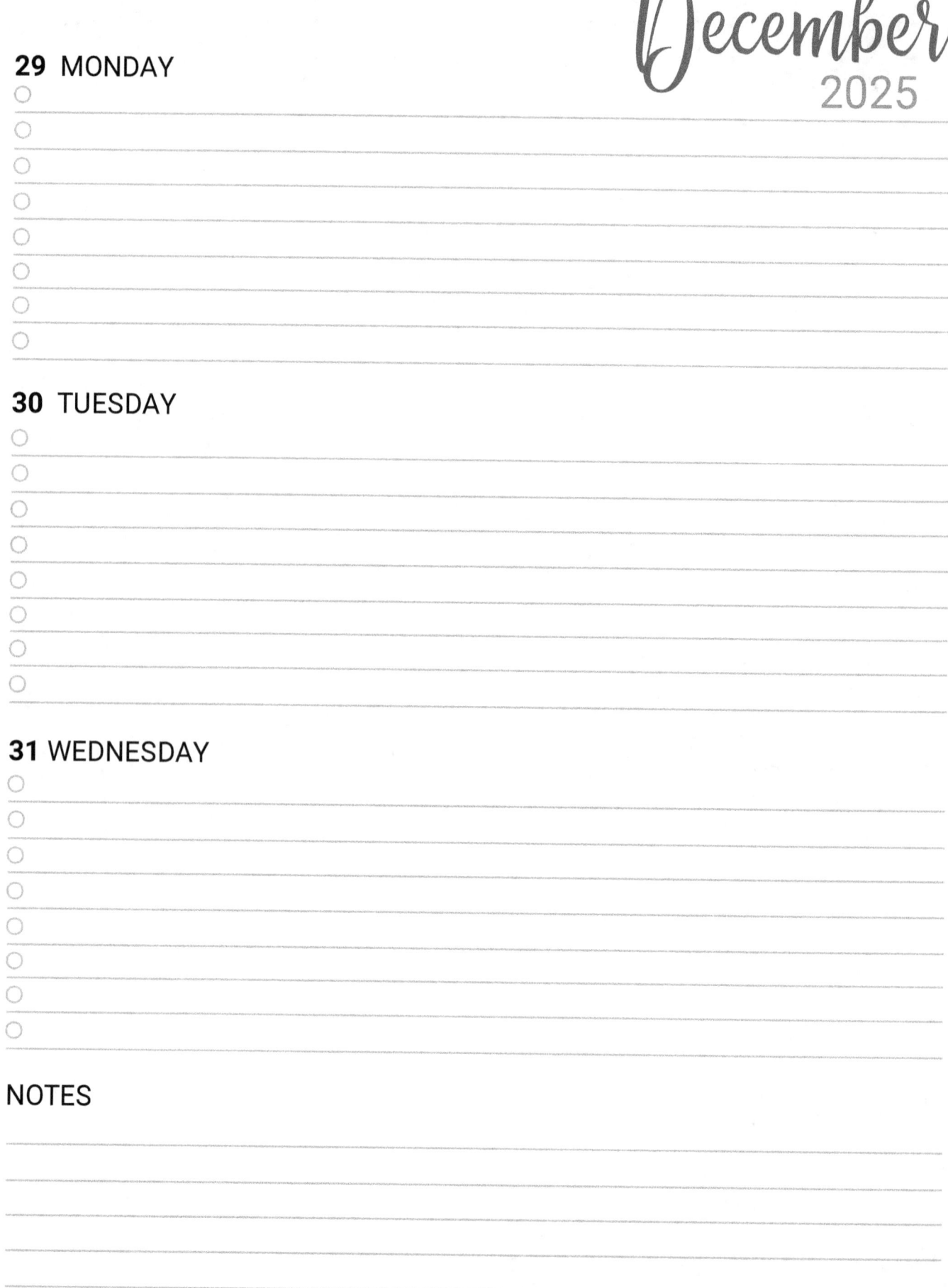

December
2025

29 MONDAY

30 TUESDAY

31 WEDNESDAY

NOTES

www.ingramcontent.com/pod-product-compliance
Lightning Source LLC
Chambersburg PA
CBHW081332120626
46546CB00011B/3322